Letters to my father

Mikayla Harris

Presentation by *BookLeaf Publishing*

Web: www.bookleafpub.com

E-mail: info@bookleafpub.com

ISBN: 9789357445108

First edition 2021

DEDICATION

To Fiona my mother, Dylan and Ronan my twin pillars and Daniel my love, you sit at the heart of all I do.

And to Michael, this one's for you Dad.

ACKNOWLEDGEMENT

Firstly I wish to thank Book Leaf Publishing for their amazing efforts to help writers create work. I'm so glad I came across this platform. Secondly to you, who is reading this right now, writers aren't much without their readers and I am grateful for you and your time. I wish to thank those closest to me who believed in me when I said I wanted to be a writer, my parents and my brothers, all my stories started with you guys.

Finally to my darling Daniel, holding my hand through everything and giving me the space to embrace all that I am, your love and belief never failing to give me the sustenance I need to keep writing.

I write for all of you.

PREFACE

We exist in a world that has become increasingly aware of itself. So transfixed on canceling all the bad, perhaps in favour of learning from it. To deny growth and the opportunity to be better is to undermine human imperfections. These aren't wrong, they are a part of what it means to live.

I started writing some of these poems before a very big occurrence in my life. A period of loss, grief, growth and an intense feeling of missing a part of something that had been with me for forever. The rest came after.

I choose to share and conquer and grow from my imperfections and mistakes, as I choose to grow from the lessons learnt by others. I always have and I always will.

So this little collection stands as a letter, or many little letters to the people in my life who I've missed, never known but wished I had, people I care about deeply, people I've learnt from, people I have grown with and grown apart from.

My writing has always been a way I could communicate my own feelings to myself. To make confusion make sense. I'm learning now as an adult to speak and write to communicate my feelings to others.

My voice is worth being heard, my words worth being read and my opinion is worth anyone's time, especially my own.

There have been people in my life who have tried to undermine my voice and my truth. To anyone who has felt this, I hope my collection of poems and prose, snapshots into my mind, my perspectives and insights can help encourage and inspire you to never stay silent.

I am inspired by you reading this. You are reading my words! The ones that I mulled over for hours, took back and changed then woke up the next morning only to put back together again.

It means something to say what you feel. Everytime you express yourself and show yourself as you truly are, it matters. You matter. In every way.

This collection is called 'Letters to my father' for a few reasons, the first is my own connection to the man who raised me and who I grow alongside every day. Another is that the idea of a father means so many different things to so many different people. I feel as though being honest and open and communicative with your father is at its core so important and yet very overlooked.

Your father might be an absent figure, a hero figure, it could be shoes that were filled by your mother. He or she might be the head of the table, the feeling you fear, the one person you wish you'd told it was okay to cry to.

The list could go on.

My hope is that you see the importance of reaching out
and saying the things you want to say, to the people you
want to say it to. To not hold on to distance or fear
because of your mistakes, or someone else's.

Write letters, have deep conversations, make someone
laugh, maybe even make someone cry and above all else
speak your truth.

Someone, somewhere is listening.

When You're Away

I'll keep your spot safe.
I'll use your cups, keep the coffee flowing.
I'll throw the ball every day,
I'll learn how to fish and help pay the bills
and do my best to keep your place warm.
Your secrets are safe with me,
Your life will be kept in peace
and in one piece.
I won't let another touch it,
or ruin the pages of your story you spent a lifetime
writing.
I'll fill the empty pages with colour, Christmas tales,
funny news stories and memories of ant and bee
and a dinosaur who went to school.
The final pages will be left blank for you to fill,
you can create your own ending.
You can change all the endings,
again and again and again.

New York

I want to tell you how New York captured my heart.
I couldn't put it into words at the time. To be in a place
you once visited, a lifetime before I touched down.
Seeing things you would have seen, the same towering
skyscrapers, the same glistening night lights, the skyline
now forever changed.
All the pictures taken with you in mind, the history only
we could talk about.
I wanted to share it with you… and the others.
Every block, every yellow taxi, all the voices, the
expanse of the great park. The pigeons and squirrels.
I felt at home and I wanted my home to be with me, to
make it perfect.
Having you there would have made it perfect.

Piano Man

You would've taught me how to play piano.
You would have listened to every song and showed me
how to read music like words, as easy as the alphabet.

You would've stopped the great depression and stopped
the great divide before their ships drifted too far apart.

With you I know nothing would've felt unfixable or
unchangeable.

The head of the table, the king of the castle.

I want you to know that your granddaughter would've
loved you beyond measure and despite never knowing
you, I still do.

You live on in our piano, in your son's smile, in your
youngest grandchild's love of music, in your oldest
grandchild's memories.

A figure I feel the presence of when I write and read.

Are you proud of me?

I feel so close to you, always closer the older I get.
I can't wait to know you true.

But I guess I'll just have to.

a writer

Pen in hand I am protected and strong.
I am worthy and whole.

The blank page is something of a miracle.

I do not fear the overwhelming need to fill it, even when
I face the block,

This means I have so much to say.

I have so much to give.

So much to learn.

This gift I have is only growing with me.

I become more and more capable every day.

The words move with me, they flow from me.

I am the creator and the artist they chose to come from.

What a wonder it is to know the pen as I do.

Missing you

Missing you is pain,
It makes me smile when I have the mind to.
To have someone to miss so badly it hurts is a blessing.
But other times it's just pain.
It's the itch you can't scratch,
The sun setting so beautifully somewhere you can't see.
It's a never ending hole,
Both numbing and aching.
In fact it aches so much my limbs do go numb.
It's a silence that roars and a space that stretches on and
on and on.
To hear your voice, see your face and make patterns out
of the freckles across your cheeks. This is what gets me
through.
Knowing I have something to miss is a wonderful
experience, still relatively new to me.
My selfish voice simply says; just never leave.
My sensible nature understands you miss me too.

Woman

She exists not only to please.
She will bring this world to its knees.

She creates without judgement or fear,
She speaks only to those who will hear.

She crumbled when you tried to break her,
But she grew, a learner but greater.

She still laughs despite the torment,
As you judge her for time well spent.

Living outside the confines of your ideals,
Feeling miracles you'll never get to feel.

She stands taller than you could even imagine.,
Sings louder and do you know what happened?

She conquered the battle you started,
She turned around and declared "I win because I'm a
woman no longer broken-hearted."

rain on the window

She had packed her bags and ran off to a place far far away.
At night she watches the rain on the window, the sound of a drenched city at midnight.
Her days are filled with coffee runs and endless hand cramps.
So at night she lets the rain wash away her pains, bathing in the glowing city lights, flickering through her window.
			Write your way to happiness.
Her mantra was also a declaration. The tool that kept her up too late and kept her mind too focused that she had forgotten how to turn it off.
Only the rain could bring calmness now, only then could she wash away her past, correct her present and predict her future.

Midnight was when the stories came to her, the ones she would keep close to her chest and nurture like a newborn baby.
The stories she was afraid to let anyone else hear or see.
They were precious to her and as delicate as each and every rain drop.

Although the hour, she never felt alone, the sounds of the streets below made her feel comforted and accepted.

She wasn't the only wandering soul awake.
She wasn't the only girl staring out her window.
She was a part of something bigger and more important
than sleep tonight or the next or the next.
She was awake because she was a link in the chain.

At midnight's rain, she was more alive than when she
was making small talk at work, or writing crappy copy
for her boss.

Minutes passed, the rain never ceased, the city breathed
and lived in the night.
		"I feel you," She whispered.
Holding her breath she could hear the city saying it back.
		Exhaling, sleep finally began to call.

My heartache

My heartache is a river,

Constantly flowing, breaking, crashing and rushing
through my body.

It leads out to the ocean only after running its course
down stream.

You can't cross the river, you can't forge through it.
Sometimes you just have to let it take you.

I hope it takes me back to you.
I hope, though battered, bruised and feeling disappointed
in myself, my heart still fits safely and perfectly in your
hands. That it doesn't slip through your fingers,
as my hold on sensibility sometimes slips through mine.

My heartache is a river, but my heart is a rock, so let it
wash over me and smooth my rough edges, until I am
soft enough to love you as we both deserve.

lost

I look around and I see empty faces,
Unfamiliar spaces and a sad place,
I don't know how I got here.

Unintended, unfortunate and unworthy.

The face in the mirror used to smile from ear to ear,
eyes lit with the wonder of uncertainty.

She used to matter to you, or at least I thought I did.

The smiles don't come so easily, not in this strange place
with strange people who tell you what you want to hear
and then take it away without a second thought.

I feel judged and humiliated, lied to and left behind.

Lost, next to people who told me they knew the way.

hey kid

I know they laughed at you and made you feel alone.
I know they convinced you to bury it inside.
You can remember the moment, the place and time, even
though the specific words evade you.

Despite this, despite them and your age; the fact that you
couldn't even explain it if you tried… you aren't alone
and you were never alone.

I wish I could go back and say "hey kid, tell me what
happened, I will listen to you and protect you as best I
can."

I wish they were stronger and that decades of fake smiles
and forgetting wasn't the natural reaction. I wish they
knew how to be better and that you realised; it wasn't
your fault that they couldn't understand you.

I wish for something that doesn't exist, but isn't that
what wishes are for?

Mostly I wish you didn't have to wait as long as you did
for someone to hear you and tell you your worth.

Who knows

When the wind blows and the rain falls, heavy in our hearts, where do we wander to?

When the sky breaks and the ground beneath us shakes, what do we hold onto?

When the trust is lost and the truth is overshadowed, who do we listen to?

When we forget who we are and where we're from, how do we find our way back?

No one tells you where to find your strength, no one can tell you or provide you with a map.

The path is too uncertain, and too long and winding to ever be the same.

But we walk it anyway and we find these things along the way.

Apologise

Just say you're sorry,
Admit you were wrong.
Along the way you lost yourself and forgot the lyrics to
our favourite song.
I won't say I told you so,
or make a big scene out of spite.
It won't cost you anything to tell us we were right.

Is your pride so important?
Your street cred unbreakable?
Who set these rules, to you so unmistakable?
You've come so far that you can no longer turn back,
But we won't hold you hostage if you just picked up the
slack.

It was never too much to ask,
Never to big a task,
Never a pain that would last,
Yet you ran away still,
Shouting 'I hate you and I always will.'
If you don't care then maybe you shouldn't come back.
If you do, just say you're sorry, it's okay to admit what
you sometimes lack.

Mother

Following footsteps and finding my feet could've been much harder.

Learning how to be, how to grow and admit the hardest truths, I didn't just learn these on my own.

You knew how to pick up the pieces and keep my heart from breaking, trusting I would fly when I touched your hand and said "let me go, I'll make it in my own way."

The softest care and the toughest advice, only a mother knows the balance.

Teach me through trial and error, through courage and earned wisdom, I want to learn.

"How did you become so strong? How do you do the things you do?"

I got it from my mother, is what I'll say.

Everything I learned, I learned from you.

the religion of you

You're like religion to me.
I've never worshipped before, a prayer here and there,
sparingly when indecision and desperation intersect.

But I go to church everyday now.
Dipping my toe into pristine holy water every morning
and night.

I shed my confessions and sins in the privacy of your
heart.

You preach not heavenly words told by prophets but
truths and confessions of your own, written in your own
hand, a holy scripture I devour; my bible I would read
over and over. Sacred, quiet, spaces created for you and
I.

Deep in conversation, wrapped up in your arms. I hear
the words you speak, from the inside out.
You make wine from water, and feed my soul with your
touch.

To walk hand in hand within your stained glass walls, I
fall to my knees and I truly believe.

what i'd tell you

if i thought you'd pick up the phone, maybe i would call you tonight, tell you about my day and the things i've been doing to keep myself busy.
if i felt like you cared, i would talk to you like we used to talk.
i sometimes have to stop myself from thinking about you everytime i watch a new tv show or see a cute tea pot. murder mysteries and a snow covered small town are your staples; how was i ever going to forget?
what would you think, how would you feel, are still questions important to me.

Every passing day, distance takes me further away from being just like you. Your face, your hair, your walk still present, just less a part of me and instead a story about who I used to be and who I used to know.

Does this make you sad, like it makes me sad?

I guess if I did call that's what I'd want to know, but I'm still not sure you would pick up the phone.

Letters to my father

Time to pick up the pieces, and let the past alone,
Silence all other voices and throw away your phone.

Life is only moving forward, but you can take one step
at a time, rewrite the story they set, as it happens line by
line.

No one gave you a map, or told you how to be, and yet
you created happiness, gave life, you created me.

It doesn't matter what they think anymore, or what tale
they want to believe, beside you are better souls, who
will stand with you and never leave.

Will these words be the be all and end all? No, you still
have strides to take yet, but a source of comfort and
peace will help make you stronger I'll bet.

Life has a funny way of telling us what we need and
you've always played a part in me learning how to be
me.

Older now and wiser from pain, let your daughter offer the same to you. See through my eyes for a spell and you'll know just what to do.

Be brave, be yourself, I wouldn't want anybody else.

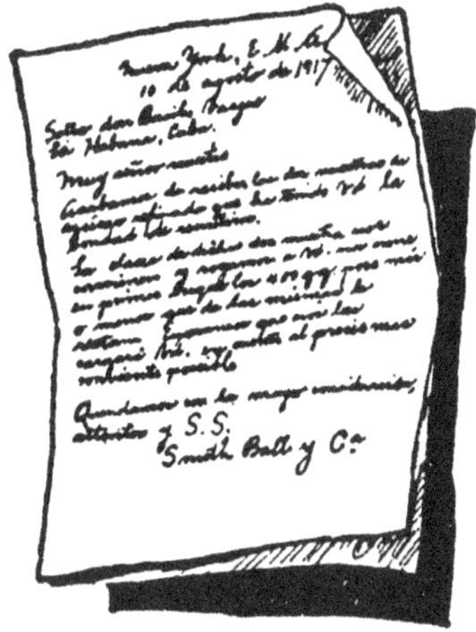

In the dark

I know I saw a light in you,
Beckoning for me to reach out, reach out, reach out,
And take it.

I held it in my hands, it was you and only you.
Soft, glowing light, so precious and beautiful, so easily
broken…

A gift it was, and a gift it still is.
If I promise not to break it, will you still shine?
Will you stay the light in the dark?

My light, my love,
my partner heart.

How lucky I am to
know the way now,
to be guided and
kept safe in the
dark.

Keep shining, keep shining,

I need to see when the fog rolls in and the darkness
hangs heavy all around me.

I know I saw a light in you, I see it there still.

It grows brighter and greater every day.

Keep shining, keep shining.

Our children

The pitter patter of little feet, the sound of our future,
Early mornings, early nights, bath times, wiggles and
messy, sticky fingers.
We shall love them more than we love ourselves and
wish them to be better than we are. Without even trying
they probably will and what a wonder that will be.

Our children, our wonderful creations, I don't know who
you are yet, what you'll be, what you'll look like, but I
hope one day you read this and know you were born to
be loved. We felt it before you were even here.
We will give you courage and kindness, we will teach
you lessons and answer all your questions. We will foster
your curiosity, because if you're anything like your
father, you will wonder about everything.
If you're like me, you will be fed creative worlds and
peaceful hours for pondering and reading.

Perhaps you're something else entirely and if we fall
short in understanding, we apologise and hope you know
that we grow every day too.

We can't wait to meet you, whenever that will be. The
thought of you someday reading this, is what keeps me
writing. This realisation I just want to share with you,
our children.

Big bears and little bears

The weather was cold and the rain incessant, but we were not going to let that spoil our fun.
Even when the power went out, we still carried on. Hide and seek, uno by candlelight, stories that sent tingles down our spines, wishing the hours would never end, wishing that the sun would never come up.

We learnt how to exist and live by learning from each other and with each other. Maybe I feel so close to empathy because of the big bear that let me play in the big kids playground with his friends, when none of my own came calling.

Maybe my strength and patience came from a little bear who needed a big sister to hold him and take care of him whenever and however he needed it, and to let it be in those times he didn't.

Maybe I found strength in watching big bears and little bears live.

Table tennis and simpsons on Saturday mornings, hours tiptoeing around rock pools and having existential conversations sitting on my bed. Quoting lines from our favourite movies and connecting through music and live performance.

Games won, games lost and hours spent in the car, silently, lost in song or taking a detour down memory lane.

Big bears, little bears, our worlds are connected. Our voices mimicking one another and our laughter mirrored.

Those that meet us go, "oh I see the resemblance now."

Brave girl

So small and kind, smart and curious, yet quiet and
timid. Your future feels so far away doesn't it?
But look at you go, look at how fast you're learning and
growing and becoming who you were meant to be.

Brave girl, you can run faster than you know and think
deeper than the ocean, you could move mountains and
topple cities to the ground if you wished it.

You don't believe you can just yet and that's okay, you
don't have to be something you're not, you don't have to
grow before your time, small steps are steps nonetheless,
don't let anyone shake your resolve.

You feel so deeply and cry so easily, not because you're
weak or easily broken, but because your soul is
connected to a higher power than what you can
physically see. You feel more than others maybe, so
don't let anyone tell you to stop crying, or to harden up.

You're already strong.

Pretty is what you were born with, but courage,
confidence and wisdom are the things you sought out
and mastered on your own.

Brave girl, live like you. Because there is no one else for
you to be.

The master

We all face disappointment in our lives, from others and from ourselves.

These are hard pills to swallow.

People change, or maybe they never were who you thought they were, but it's not your fault, and you weren't a fool to believe in them.

Sometimes, "I'll be there for you" means very little and people don't show up.

Sometimes you will be left to pick yourself up.

Sometimes you will be alone.

Sometimes vulnerability will let love in, and your life will never be the same.

People will surprise you and you will surprise yourself, standing so tall and sure of who you are.

Disappointment becomes a lesson, you understand you're here to learn as much as live. Boundaries are set, not walls to lock out hope or trust, but ivy-covered

fences separating your home from the wrecking ball that
tried to knock you down.
This is your space - your life and it's your responsibility
to protect and take care of.

Let the pain be a part of your journey, not a reason to
end the story.

When a friend becomes a foe,
When brother turns on brother,
When a son forgets where his home used to be,
When a childhood is lost,
When hidden pain comes with consequences…

Learn, live, love again and trust again, in your own way,
at your own pace.

You don't become something or someone when you get
older, you're always growing from zero to the very end.

Once we understand this; mistakes, loss, disappointment
and life itself becomes easier and you become the master
of your own being.

As you deserve.